GOOD OL'
SNOOPY

GOOD OL'

SNOOPY

Selected Cartoons from
SNOOPY VOL. II

Charles M. Schulz

FAWCETT CREST • NEW YORK

GOOD OL' SNOOPY

This book, prepared especially for Fawcett Crest Books, a unit of CBS Publications, the Consumer Publishing Division of CBS Inc., comprises the second half of SNOOPY, and is reprinted by arrangement with Holt, Rinehart and Winston, Inc.

ISBN: 0-449-23709-5

Printed in the United States of America.

57   56   55   54   53   52   51   50

THE FLOOD WATERS ARE RISING!!

SCHULZ

EXCUSE ME..I THINK SOMEBODY'S
WATER DISH IS EMPTY

HERE COMES THE BIG POLAR BEAR STALKING ACROSS THE SNOW!

I'LL BET **REAL** POLAR BEARS NEVER GET COLD!

Schulz

WHAT A TEAM! GOOD GRIEF!!

I'VE GOT A CATCHER WHO CAN'T SEE, A FIRST BASEMAN WHO'S ONLY THREE FEET TALL, AND AN OUTFIELDER WHO CAN'T THROW!

CAN'T THROW? I'VE NEVER HEARD OF SUCH A THING...

WELL, NOW YOU HAVE!

SCHULZ

HERE COMES THE BIG ELEPHANT, TROMPING THROUGH THE JUNGLE...

TROMP! TROMP! TROMP!

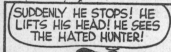

SUDDENLY HE STOPS! HE LIFTS HIS HEAD! HE SEES THE HATED HUNTER!

TROMP TROMP TROMP TROMP   TROMP TROMP TROMP TROMP

SOMETIMES I WISH I WERE A RHINOCEROS!

THEN I WOULDN'T HAVE TO TAKE ANYTHING FROM ANYBODY! I COULD JUST GO AROUND BUMPING PEOPLE..

AH! A VICTIM!

BUMP BUMP BUMP

?

YOU CLOSE YOUR EYES, SNOOPY, AND I'LL HIDE THE BALL..

OH, C'MON...YOU'RE PEEKING.. CLOSE 'EM ALL THE WAY!

CLOSE THEM ALL THE WAY, AND THEN COVER THEM UP...

SCHULZ

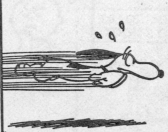

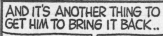

CIRCUS DOGS DON'T STEP ON THEIR OWN EARS..

YIPE!!

THE WORST THING A PERSON CAN DO IS WASTE HIS LIFE HANGING AROUND STREET CORNERS!

WELL! THERE HE IS!

MY PAL!!

EVERYONE SHOULD HAVE A DOG TO GREET HIM WHEN HE COMES HOME!

THAT'S THE ONLY PENGUIN IN THE WORLD WITH LONG BLACK EARS!

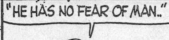